David Cottrell
President and CEO

I Quit, But Forgot to Tell You

Dear Valued Client:

We've all seen it…and it's devastating when it happens…employees who are physically present but who have mentally checked out.

Let's face it. No one takes a job planning to fail. Likewise, no one hires with the intent to eventually fire. Both parties want to succeed. So, what happens between an employee's first day and their last?

I Quit, But Forgot to Tell You examines the virus of disengagement and provides some real-world antidotes to prevent this plague from contaminating your entire organization.

I Quit, But Forgot to Tell You can transform your management team and the way they motivate their team members. Loaded with ideas and recommendations, this book will enable your management staff to achieve the goals of your organization…and more!

Providing this book for every manager, supervisor and team leader could be one of the best investments you will make this year. It can make a difference in employee morale, motivation and your bottom line!

Best wishes for prosperity in all your endeavors,

David Cottrell

P.S. A downloadable PowerPoint presentation to help you teach your team these principles is available at www.CornerStoneLeadership.com.

P.O. Box 764087 • Dallas, Texas 75376
Phone: 888-789-LEAD • FAX: 1-972-274 2884
www.cornerstoneleadership.com

I Quit,

But Forgot
to Tell You

Attacking the

Spreading Virus of

Disengagement

TERRI KABACHNICK

NEW AND CONDENSED VERSION
Edited and condensed by Emily Crawford

I Quit,
But Forgot
to Tell You

Inquiries regarding permission for use of the material contained in this book should be addressed to:

CornerStone Leadership Institute
P.O. Box 764087
Dallas, TX 75376
888.789.LEAD

Printed in the United States of America
ISBN: 0-9772257-9-8

Credits

Cover Design	Yoori Kim Designs
Interior design, art direction, and production	Melissa Monogue, Back Porch Creative, Plano, TX info@BackPorchCreative.com

No one takes a job intending to fail. No employer hires with the intent to fire. Both parties want only the best. So what happens? The virus of employee disengagement attacks and spreads.

INTRODUCTION

Many companies are suffering from poor productivity and profits. The cause? Disengaged workers, a costly virus that's spreading throughout businesses worldwide.

Let's face it, both employees and employers want to succeed. So what happens? Disengagement statistics are telling, but they don't convey the entire story. You must look at the human issues behind the numbers. For that reason, much of this book is premised on my professional experiences with many organizations in a variety of industries.

I left retailing to start The Kabachnick Group (TKG) with a mission to teach service-oriented businesses what I had so vividly come to learn – how to develop customer loyalty through employees. A CEO of one our largest clients said something to me that changed my business focus and me. *"Terri, I'm tired of spending all this money on training…only to have people leave and take your great training elsewhere. We need to change what we're doing."*

His comments ignited a revolutionary moment for me. He was dead right. No amount of training would ever change an employee who did not believe in the concept of service and servicing others.

That moment made a critical difference in my business approach. I changed from simply training to selecting and retaining the *right* people to train and develop.

Understanding that selecting and retaining the right people up-front inspired our research and the content of this book. We have surveyed, interviewed, assessed, analyzed or studied more than 44 organizations with more than 6,500 employees at all levels.

We learned that behaviors and beliefs are cross-cultural. People are people – each with their own biases, prejudices, and issues. Yet, they want to grow and do a good job.

Given the ever-changing factors in today's talent pool, managing human inventory is every bit as important – if not more than – as managing product inventory. Why? Because, in reality, people are companies and companies are its people.

It's now time for organizations to apply technological and common sense tools to manage and engage people and their development.

The concepts in this book are premised on real-life business experiences. The ideas and recommendations are straightforward, logical truths that apply to every industry and every organization. They are practical tools, techniques and tactics proven to diffuse disengagement whenever it occurs.

It's up to you to step into the driver's seat, make use of these tools and accept responsibility for your own destiny and that of your employees.

Read it. Use it to reinvigorate, reinforce and re-engage your workforce!

CONTENTS

(1)

DETACHED, DISHEARTENED AND DISCONNECTED – DO THEY WORK FOR YOU?

A s customers, we have been "served" by people who quit but never left. As employees, we have been managed by bosses who quit but managed to stay. As managers, we have managed people who physically attend but mentally pretend.

Far too many companies suffer from the tremendous cost of employee turnover and what they must do to retain valuable workers. Retention remains a critical challenge for all businesses, but it's time to redefine the term. We must examine the reasons for retention, as well as its benefits and costs, and realize that the virus of disengagement is spreading throughout the workplace – usually faster than turnover.

TO RETAIN OR NOT

Retention is not a cure for turnover. Retaining a disengaged employee is far worse than letting him go – regardless of how valuable he once was. Far too much time and money is wasted on training workshops and seminars teaching disengaged workers how to "talk the talk," when in the end, they won't "walk the walk." Instead, we must learn to recognize disengaged workers before we waste more time and money in futile attempts to change them.

Why do employees become disengaged? The Kabachnick Group's (TKG) research has pinpointed the very soul of disengagement:

O Most disengaged workers were once engaged, caring workers.

O Disengaged workers are not necessarily poor performers.

O Disengagement usually begins with either a new boss or a boss who becomes disengaged.

O Disengagement often occurs after changes in the responsibilities of a position.

O Disengagement can set in after a promotion.

O Disengagement begins when learning and development end.

The reasons for disengagement are both economic and behavioral. Mentally leaving a job where you're unhappy but guaranteed a paycheck might be better than having no job at all. Money motivates disengaged workers to stick with the jobs they hate. Behavioral factors are an even more powerful motivator.

Target Training International (TTI) research reveals that 42% of North Americans possess a behavior style that prefers a work environment of steadiness, little change, predictability and consistency – routine work with little interruption. Other characteristics of this style include avoiding confrontation, passive disagreements and a preference for sameness. In other words, "I may be unhappy, I may complain, but only to friends and co-workers. I may think of leaving – eventually –

but I'll stew in my frustrations until something better comes along."

Without a manager who understands this style and recognizes the early signs of disengagement, this worker may meet all of the criteria for becoming a fully disengaged worker and thus costing the employer in time and money.

THE COST OF DISENGAGEMENT

All disengaged workers are not the same. Yet the cost of different forms of disengagement is relatively equal in size: Huge!

Employee emotions drive disengagement. They are triggered by the attitudes, values and beliefs of their leaders, which in turn govern how the leaders treat their employees.

During the course of an organizational survey, Suzanne, a district sales manager in her late 30s, was confidentially explaining to me why her colleagues were concerned about her loss of enthusiasm and involvement. Suzanne's comments were honest, simple and insightful. "My heart's just not in it anymore." Suzanne was a bright, fast-rising star when she first started with the company. She was given a variety of challenges, the results of which were either supported with recognition and praise or constructive coaching. She welcomed both because she was learning and growing. When the new boss arrived, the learning ended. Conversations became one-sided and focused only on numbers. She was told to "keep up the good work." She did. Then, several months later, without any recognition for her outstanding results, she was simply given a bigger district to manage. Fortunately, an intervention program that included coaching both Suzanne and her boss prevented her disengagement from spreading and negatively affecting business results. Suzanne was a terrific employee who needed to be retained and "saved." Several months later she was recognized, promoted and has continued to rise in her leadership role.

At another company, TKG uncovered that disengagement was taking a toll on company-wide motivation, productivity and customer service, even though the percentage of disengaged employees was fairly small. Two disengaged managers were adversely affecting supervisors and employees, causing these workers to have a "why bother" attitude about servicing customers. Over time, falling sales figures and low service scores caused a negative reaction within the entire district, plummeting it from number one to number five. Two disengaged managers had dramatically impacted hundreds of workers and caused a notable decline in an entire district.

EIGHT FATEFUL REASONS OF DISENGAGEMENT

From studies conducted in many organizations, TKG identified eight fateful reasons for disengagement. They are:

1. **Job-Employee Mismatch:** Resumes are written to "sell" a job candidate and often resemble advertisements. They're not always accurate. References, who are afraid of repercussions, are not always truthful and forthcoming. As a result, applicants are hired because of what they claim to have done in the past rather than what they can and will do in the future. Jobs are defined by tasks to be done rather than by the behaviors, values and attributes required for success.

2. **Overworked and Under Appreciated:** People become disengaged because of a heavy workload, long hours and a lack of appreciation. Many times management recognizes the high performers with more tasks to perform, and the occasional "Atta Boy" or complimentary lunches are insufficient recognition.

3. **Culture Shock:** Cultures often change when companies merge.

Workers do not receive sufficient communication, rumors run rampant, and people begin to believe that they no longer "fit," especially when management fails to prepare them for the new order.

A media/printing company had a very casual dress code that matched their clients' standards. The company merged with another firm that required every manager to wear a suit and tie. After 12 years of corporate casual attire, many of the managers didn't even own suits. Following the merger, management gave no reasons for the new dress code. They simply changed the policy. Almost immediately, one of the top performers – recognized by colleagues as a natural leader – sent an e-mail that read: "Do you believe this sh**t? We're going back to the dark ages. I'm outta here!" Two weeks later, he took a job with a competitor. What followed was a chain of emigration. And to make matters worse, some of the best managers who jumped ship also took their support people with them. Much of this could have been avoided had there been better communication.

Note: Your good people typically are the first to leave. They're the ones with the most confidence and a proven track record. They know they're talented and that the odds of getting a new job are good.

4. **Politics and Perception:** One of the most frequent irritants to employees is the perception that managers play favorites. It's one of the primary causes of disengagement. Do managers intentionally play favorites? In some cases, yes. But for most, it's simply a matter of liking some people more than others – a natural human outcome. Often, it's demonstrated through informal socializing or nothing more than having small talk with those he feels comfortable with while talking only business with others. Small talk makes a big difference and

is an important part of establishing rapport. Managers need to establish rapport with all of their people, not just some.

5. **Politics and Control:** Some managers – usually new hires – make it known that they intend to fire existing employees to make room for "their own people." This attitude has more to do with comfort, allegiance, payback and insecurity than politics. It is irrational behavior that causes the loss of valuable talent. Senior executives should be suspicious when new managers report that previous top players have suddenly turned "bad."

6. **The "Peter Principle:"** People do not consciously accept job promotions because they hope to "rise to the level of their incompetence." They accept promotions because it's the route to a better salary and benefits. Everyone could use extra money. But could everyone use additional responsibilities and workload, especially if they're happy where they are and/or believe the promotion will lead to their downfall? If you ask the average worker, "Would you like new responsibilities?" the mindset is usually, "If I don't accept, I'm history. I can't pass up the promotion." Rather than accept unwanted promotions, the best people leave. Those who stay become disengaged, whether they accept the promotion or not. That's because the "target for promotion" is often given more work anyway, which breeds resentment.

7. **Business "By the Book:"** Too many companies favor adherence to rules, guidelines and processes over creativity and flexibility. It's easier to run a business with rules and regulations than to encourage innovation, individual contributions and compromise. There's no thinking required: just do as you're told. "Follow these procedures, comply with these policies, order goods this

way, send goods that way. Left, right, left, right." This is not to say that policies and procedures are not valuable and necessary. But, as companies and business climates change, management must seek out new ideas and rely on genuine teamwork instead of simply paying lip service to the few who follow the rules.

8. **The "Bad" Boss:** Disengagement is as much about managers as it is frontline workers. While the bad employee may affect his co-workers, the bad manager causes more widespread damage and disengagement among employees and other managers.

Workers can become disengaged for one or a number of these fateful reasons. And once their disengagement sets in, it spreads quickly. Retaining a disengaged employee is far worse than letting him go. We must learn to recognize disengaged workers before we waste more time and money in futile attempts to change them.

2

FOR PROFITS, YOU NEED PEOPLE
WHO PERFORM. PERIOD!

The number one issue facing businesses is finding and retaining *productive* employees. In fact, TKG found that 75% of the demand for new employees is fueled by the need to replace workers who have left the company.

In a Kabachnick Group survey of more than 800 managers, 76% admitted that low employee productivity is their single greatest job challenge. A few underlying reasons for this "challenge" are:

- ○ 72% of management has failed to acquire interviewing, hiring and profiling skills.

- ○ Only 22% of companies measure turnover and hold managers accountable for the results.

- ○ 83% of managers hire people they "like" rather than what the job requires.

○ 82% of managers refer to frontline employees as "coverage."

○ Less than one-third of these companies use hiring tools, position competencies, job profiles, behaviors and beliefs or selling/service assessments.

The bottom line: For profits, you need people who perform. Productivity, engagement and retention are overwhelmingly people issues.

A study by Bain & Company in Boston found that successful companies have two common traits:

1. A high percentage of repeat business

2. Low levels of employee turnover

Regardless of size, the companies in the Bain study were vastly more profitable than their competitors. Their leaders recognized that loyalty – internal and external – is a better profit forecaster than market share, cost position or quality of service. If you want higher profits, you aim for customer and employee loyalty.

DO YOUR EMPLOYEES LOVE WHAT THEY DO BUT NOT WHERE THEY DO IT?

According to a TKG survey of 1,400 executives, managers and associates (of all ages), 84% of people enjoy what they do but not where they do it.

Specifically, they cite company policies that inhibit creativity, rules and procedures that make no sense and executives who live on a planet called entitlement. Such complaints may seem unrelated, but often they combine to produce a negative synergy that promotes employee resentment and disengagement.

I once worked with a small-business owner whose 25-person workforce was experiencing "morale issues." Specifically, many employees resented what they perceived as the CEO's ostentatious displays of personal wealth. After conducting assessments, I traced the true source of the problem: the CEO focused on every mistake made by employees and provided almost no recognition of their accomplishments.

The "personal wealth" issue never manifested itself until the CEO began focusing on worker mistakes. It was only then that employees began trading e-mails about the boss's new luxury car, expensive vacations, etc. It was only then that "planet entitlement" became the focus of employee discontent.

One manager in shipping said, "I asked for a new computer that would help me track inventory better, and I couldn't get it. Another said, "I wanted to buy a laptop because I found that I could be doing a lot more work at home. They wouldn't buy me one, but the boss went ahead and spent money on a very expensive media center for his office."

This is an example of how the virus of disengagement begins to rear its ugly head. Executive compensation is rarely the root cause of employee discontent. But workers' day-to-day grievances can become intertwined with any management behavior or decision, making it the focus of anger and resentment.

BE A COMPANY OF GIANTS

A physics professor, who earned his Ph.D. some 20 years ago, made this statement in a speech: "More than half of the correct answers I gave on my finals 20 years ago are no longer true. What we have learned in science in the past 20 years has yielded new truths that didn't exist then."

We understand this in science, but not when it comes to people. We need to update our people quotient and build upon new truths to foster engagement in the workplace. In the not-so-distant past, many people worked at jobs they hated because they believed there were no choices. A job was something you had to do. You weren't supposed to enjoy it.

Thankfully, this attitude is changing rapidly. Today, we understand that motivation – and therefore engagement – comes from loving what you do. You love what you do when you are in the right job, feel valued and are given opportunities to grow. Get your people to love what they do, and they are yours – fully engaged.

"If each of us hires people who are smaller than we are, we shall become a company of dwarves. But if each of us hires people who are bigger than we are, we will become a company of giants."

David Ogilvy,
advertising mogul

BEFORE YOU BEGIN,
BEGIN WITH YOU

Y**ou know a disengaged worker. He is your colleague, your direct report or the cashier at the local supermarket. He is any employee, the manager, or he could be you.**

Disengaged workers hide in plain sight, infecting departments, divisions and entire companies with a virus that promotes poor productivity, resentment and outright sabotage. People and profits give in to this disease, and so does customer loyalty – a critical resource that, once lost, is hard to restore.

According to a recent Gallup poll, disengaged workers cost U.S. based organizations more than $250 billion a year. Our own research has found that as many as 65% of all employees are disengaged.

It is important to note that disengagement and low morale are not the same. Low morale occurs when a caring, engaged worker becomes frustrated with his supervisors, workload, environment, company policies, etc. Poor morale can lead to disengagement, but disengagement itself occurs after the employee has ceased to care. He has mentally checked out and emotionally divorced himself from the organization.

The symptoms of disengagement are very commonplace. They are often so seemingly trivial that most managers fail to recognize them until the patient is "terminal." Many managers misdiagnose employee issues, attributing problems to lack of training, teamwork, leadership or communication. Still others avoid dealing with any "people issues," preferring denial to confrontation.

Are you engaged or disengaged? It's important to begin with yourself.

When you're disengaged at work…

　○ What kind of co-worker are you?

　○ What kind of manager are you?

　○ What kind of leader are you?

　○ What kind of friend are you?

　○ What kind of spouse are you?

　○ What kind of parent are you?

Take a few minutes to measure your own engagement quotient. Take the Engaging Quiz by circling the answers that best apply to you, and then calculate the total number of true responses. Being absolutely candid will be the best gift you can give yourself to learn your engagement quotient.

AN ENGAGING QUIZ
(T = True, F = False, NS = Not Sure)

1. My boss cares about me as a person.   (T, F, NS)

2. My opinion counts.   (T, F, NS)

3. I know what is expected of me at work.   (T, F, NS)

4. I am clear on my purpose within my organization.   (T, F, NS)

5. I usually volunteer for projects. I enjoy the challenge
   of something new.   (T, F, NS)

6. I feel comfortable alerting my boss before he or she
   is about to make an embarrassing decision.   (T, F, NS)

7. My personal development is an important objective
   for my boss.   (T, F, NS)

8. Every day I have an opportunity to do what I do best.   (T, F, NS)

9. My boss has no people who are "favorites."   (T, F, NS)

10. If I felt disconnected with my boss, I could definitely
    broach the subject with him or her.   (T, F, NS)

11. I have the necessary support and materials to do
    my job well.   (T, F, NS)

12. Our organization identifies and handles poor
    performers quickly.   (T, F, NS)

13. Everyone is held to the same standards of performance
    and behavior.   (T, F, NS)

14. I am encouraged to interface with other departments and develop proactive relationships. (T, F, NS)

15. I have clear goals and expectations by which my performance is evaluated. (T, F, NS)

16. I have a written plan for personal development – one approved and supported by my boss. (T, F, NS)

17. I am receiving adequate skills training and coaching. (T, F, NS)

18. I have a trusted mentor. (T, F, NS)

19. I have access to role models within my organization. (T, F, NS)

20. I talk about my work in a truly honest and positive way to my friends and family. (T, F, NS)

TOTAL TRUE:

15 – 20 True – You are *Truly Engaged*

10 – 14 True – You are *Mostly Engaged*

9 or fewer True – You are *Not Quite Engaged*

Engaged leaders are committed to personal and professional growth, both for themselves and their people.

GUIDELINES FOR TACKLING YOUR OWN DISENGAGEMENT:

Assess your beliefs about your job – Do you love what you do? Do you love where you work? Work should be a source of energy, not exhaustion. If your job is not satisfying, your behaviors may be revealing how you truly feel about your job. You may have to change your behaviors or do yourself and everyone else a favor: QUIT!

Adapt and adjust your behaviors to suit each individual you manage. Understand your personal communication preferences and work style. Be aware of and understand other people's individual preferences. How does your approach to work and communication differ from those around you? Don't try to change workers' habits to fit your perception of how a job must be done. Respect individual techniques and methods, unless they are detrimental to the job or the business. The reward is a motivated, self-directed worker who feels confident and worthy. To be an engaged leader or manager, learn to adapt your style to that of others.

Pay attention to your best employees. These are the people whom managers have a tendency to ignore because they're busy focusing on problem employees. Consider the advantages of improving a top performer's productivity by just 10% rather than improving the performance of a mediocre worker by 10%. Also, keep in mind that the best employees are usually the first to leave.

React to poor performers quickly. Your employees know before you do who is slacking off on the job and not contributing. Make it easy and safe for caring employees to come to you with concerns about other employees' work habits. Ask for facts and keep it confidential. Then act on the information!

Pay attention to the little things. Figure out how to say "thank you" to your star performers in unique ways. One company employs part-timers as "assistants" to run errands for top-performing employees. They perform various tasks – from picking up dry cleaning to grocery shopping. The result is increased productivity achieved by top performers once they're freed from a few tasks. You may or may not agree with this unique approach, but it works extremely well for this company.

Create a greenhouse for employees to grow. Foster an environment that nourishes each individual's interests, skill development and desire to learn. Encourage workers to set goals and to dream. Then, give them the tools to reach their goals. Just like healthy, flourishing plants need food, water and care, people need care and nurturing too!

Think with your heart. Put yourself in your employees' shoes. Do you know what they like that would make them feel good? We're talking about freshly baked cookies for afternoon breaks, or in-house shoulder and foot massages. Sound silly? It's not. Employees may work for the compensation, but they stay because of the supervisor and the environment the company creates. A top-performing salesperson – with annual sales over $1.5 million – receives two to three headhunter calls per week. She says, "It's not the money that keeps me here. I could probably make more elsewhere, but could I find another boss who cares about me and my feet?"

4

BUSINESS IS PEOPLE

Consider what it means to be engaged. It means that a person is involved, occupied, committed, meshed, participating. The most significant attribute of the engaged employee is that she is "unavailable" to anyone else – meaning other employers.

When fully engaged in her work, her energy and focus are laser-directed to outcomes and satisfaction. Results become rewards, producing euphoric feelings that boost self-esteem and provide a sense of control over one's destiny.

Engaged workers believe the grass is greener on *their* side. They would not think of leaving. They become a company's strongest asset – one that cannot be wooed, tempted away or stolen.

Film directors know that engaged actors, ones who believe in the project, can transform even mediocre scripts into Oscar-winning movies. On the other hand, disengaged performers can send screen gems into oblivion. The best of all worlds occurs when every player in the production works together to produce an engaged synergy – to create a product that is greater than the sum of its parts. In other words, engaged people drive the success of an enterprise.

Companies are only as good as their people because companies are their people.

It's an obvious statement but, in practice, too few business owners and managers recognize employee contributions to the bottom line. Management tends to view labor as overhead – a necessary expense – rather than the source of sales, revenues and profits. While it's true that many organizations reward star performers, most take their supporting players for granted. As a result, the consistent, reliable soldiers who spend each day in the trenches getting the job done are ignored.

Any discussion of employee engagement must include recognition of employees as human beings with lives, problems and challenges that will and do affect their work. Many business leaders were raised in an environment where "life" was supposed to be separate from work, with personal and professional lives stored in neat, non-intersecting compartments. The "disconnects" caused by compartmentalization and by refusing to deal with "squishy" people issues, are prime catalysts of worker disengagement.

Consider the following real-life example:

Paul, an executive from a chain retailer, spent significant sums of money hiring and relocating Phil, a top merchandise manager from another company who was responsible for huge volumes and profitable margins. Phil was excited about the move but was also excited about the imminent birth of twin boys. Six months passed since Phil was offered the assignment and he moved to the new location with his family.

Paul called me about the same time. "I don't know what happened," he said. "Phil was one of the best in the industry. We invested so much time and money to bring him into the company. He was fired up and involved. I don't know what's happening. He comes in late. His enthusiasm's gone and he's withdrawn. I don't know what's changed."

I asked Paul if he had spoken with Phil about what he saw. Paul replied that he had and Phil had assured him that everything was fine. Phil said he was just adjusting to a new culture and new people. But, obviously, something wasn't fine and, whatever it was, Phil wasn't talking about it. "Frankly," said Paul, "if he's got issues with his wife or whatever, I don't want to know about it."

Phil agreed to take an assessment and meet with me for a debriefing. "Some discrepancies in the assessment tell me that you're dealing with difficult issues — that you're under a lot of stress," I suggested. With little resistance, Phil admitted as much, and with my promise that our discussion would remain confidential, he opened up.

Phil's twin boys were born with a brain deficiency and had been given a year to 18 months to live. Can you imagine how unbearable Phil's situation must have been? Returning home every night to two baby boys who carried a death sentence?

With empathy, I exclaimed, "Phil, you never said anything to Paul about the boys?" "No," he replied. "I don't want anybody to feel sorry for me."

I asked, "Do you realize you're no longer the same person you were six months ago? People see the change, and they're speculating reasons that have nothing to do with reality. Don't you think you're doing yourself and others a great disservice?"

Phil's response was adamant. "I told you that I don't want Paul to know about this and feel sorry for me. Besides, I know Paul doesn't want to deal with anything that isn't work related."

This example vividly illustrates how the personal and professional worlds can intersect, causing even the best employees to become disengaged. Phil's disengagement was caused by a family crisis, one that made it understandably impossible for him to focus on the job. And because Paul wanted to hear about nothing except "work-related issues," the situation had intensified, leading to a total misunderstanding.

BE PROFESSIONALLY PERSONAL

In such situations, in order to discover the "roots of disengagement," I recommend that the boss get to know more about the person first, then get to know the issues. I'm not suggesting that managers become amateur therapists, but I do recommend a show of compassion, empathy and flexibility. Display a professionally personal attitude.

○ Ask appropriate questions and don't ignore personal situations.

○ Listen actively to understand and suggest ways that you, in your professional capacity, can help the employee.

○ Direct employees to appropriate sources of information and assistance.

○ Support a leave of absence, schedule vacation time or work out a flexible schedule.

Business IS people. People have lives. Lives have problems. Deal with them. Avoidance is NOT the solution.

RECOGNIZE THE EMERGING ATTITUDES TOWARD WORK

Today, employees are quietly rebelling. They are creating shifts within companies that remind me of the beach erosions caused by storms. No matter how well developers plan and execute, nature eventually determines the landscape.

Human nature, like any natural system, is powerful and complex. It can strike with deadly force or it can slowly and systematically change the landscape. Such is the case for managers. Today's workers are slowly altering the workplace through their behavior. Deeply held beliefs about independence, life-balance and individualism support their actions.

Some experts attribute these beliefs and behaviors to generational differences. I believe that the emerging attitudes are a cross-generational response to life's changing demands. By studying and understanding these trends, managers can help redefine employee roles and better manage their people power.

CONSIDER QUALITY OF LIFE

Do your people work to live or live to work? Many older managers believe younger workers have a poor work ethic. Younger workers say, "Get a life," and refuse to become entangled in an "unbalanced existence." Meanwhile, younger managers face difficulties with older workers who are unwilling to accept change.

In many organizations, I've observed that both sets of workers are quietly influencing each other. They recognize similarities and overlaps in their beliefs. Older workers often regret having paid excessive "dues" at the expense of family and happiness. They now want a fuller life. Younger workers want to control the work that shapes their lives.

They want flexibility. They have evolved hybrid values, beliefs and behaviors that revolve around quality-of-life issues.

A Kabachnick Group survey of 1,400 executives, managers and associates (of all ages) reveals some specific beliefs:

- ○ 76% would switch jobs for less money in order to work for a company that offers personal development and flexibility.

- ○ 58% believe that an outsider has a better chance of getting the job or promotion that they want.

- ○ 81% believe the way to the top is strictly political.

EMPLOYEE DEVELOPMENT IS KEY

Today, self-development is the single largest contributor to job satisfaction. Employees will choose one employer over another when the company provides more training and development.

The Container Store, voted by *Fortune Magazine* as one of the Top Ten employers for several consecutive years, is an employer of choice. This successful retailer provides training for every employee each year that is over five times the industry average – and it shows in their service and bottom line. Contrast that with the 30 hours a year that is the average for the industry.

Sadly, many managers believe an employee's desire for training and career development is influenced by an ulterior motive. In other words, "Once you provide me with adequate training, I'll take these skills to another (better) employer."

It's a valid concern. But ask yourself this question: How much will it cost if you choose not to develop your people? Or consider this fact based on an Accenture/Deloitte study: The typical U.S. company spends almost 50 times more to recruit a $100,000 worker than it will invest in his annual training after he joins the company.

When you develop people to the highest standards, they will not want to leave. In most cases, leaving a company for a higher salary is merely an excuse. Actually, one of the top reasons people leave their jobs is directly tied to their relationship with their boss. TKG research shows that an employee's performance will move 30 percent positively or negatively, all based on the environment. The boss creates that environment.

5

THE VIRAL PROGRESSION
OF DISENGAGEMENT

Why would a senior executive allow a bad employee to remain on the job for two years – the average time it takes a manager to deal with an actively disengaged employee?

The progression from engagement to disengagement cycles through **five distinct phases**, and if any of these phases goes unrecognized, it can cause many disengaged workers to appear "healthy," even though they are spreading the virus to others.

The virus grows in stages. As individuals move through the stages of disengagement, there will be recognizable symptoms as well as identifiable timelines.

PHASE 1 – *The Honeymoon Phase – Engaged – 3 to 6 months*
The individual is excited, eager to learn and produce results. The

employee looks forward to new relationships and new challenges with co-workers and customers. She listens to and observes her managers closely. She wants to know, see and feel what works and what doesn't.

The highest turnover occurs in this phase, usually because the employee realizes that the job is not what she expected.

PHASE 2 – *The Impressionable Phase – Actively Engaged – 1 year*

Now the employee has a sense of what is expected and has discovered which tasks she may not like or not perform well. How well the manager provides feedback and communicates responsibilities and expectations will impact how the employee views her job. She will either like it and will want to learn more or she'll start to question why she accepted the job in the first place.

Unless managed poorly, the employee normally maintains self-motivation and job interest. It is in Phase 2 that managers make the mistake of incorrectly assuming that the "good worker" does not require much input or attention. With effective management, an employee remains in this stage much longer.

PHASE 3 – *The Comparing Phase – Limbo – Up to 2 years*

At this point the employee is assimilated and trained. If Phase 2 worked well, she's motivated, confident and productive. She wants to continue learning, developing and contributing to the organization. But, if Phase 2 was mismanaged, she becomes infected with the disengagement virus, and the first symptoms of disengagement begin to appear. The employee begins to compare her situation to that of other workers, looks for negatives and wonders about her future with the company.

If management does not pay attention to this individual's needs, the employee will move into Phase 4.

PHASE 4 – *The Intervention Phase – Reactively Disengaged – Average of 18 months*

Without management intervention in Phase 3, she becomes reactively disengaged. The manager will notice unusual behavior and/or poor performance, including tardiness, a lack of involvement, excessive socializing and sloppy, late or indifferent work. Absenteeism, tardiness and a "who cares" attitude becomes apparent.

This is the stage where a manager's involvement, coaching and counseling are critical for improving motivation, performance and the likelihood of retention.

PHASE 5 – *The Critical Phase – Actively Disengaged – 9 months*

Once the employee reaches active disengagement, the employee is usually beyond "redemption." She becomes disruptive and unproductive. By now she has infected others in a negative way, and it would be an impossible feat for her to retract everything she's complained about and adopt a positive attitude.

During down time, she will degrade management, complain about perceived slights, criticize co-workers' behaviors and try to prevent others from doing what is right. Anger and resentment dominate her workplace emotions, causing you, the manager, to avoid her, especially if you dislike confrontation.

Unless fired, she will continue to infect everyone with whom she interacts. She will encourage unproductive, disruptive and sometimes rebellious behavior.

DON'T WAIT – DIAGNOSE NOW

Be attentive to your employees and look for symptoms of disengagement early in Phase 2.

Focus on those mired in Phase 3. Meet with them to answer the following:

○ Is the employee naturally suited for the job? Assessments of behavior, values and attributes will provide the insights to make a well-informed decision.

○ Would the employee benefit from being placed in another position or location, or with a different manager?

○ If the employee is suited for the job, then ask this question: "We both know you're not as productive and happy as you could be in the job. How can I help?" Say nothing more. Listen and wait for the employee to talk.

Employees who reach Phase 4 are typically doing only what has to be done and involving others in their unhappiness. This phase requires immediate management involvement and, in most cases, disciplinary action. Reactive (hidden) disengagement will morph into active disengagement.

Once active disengagement – Phase 5 - has been reached, it's too late. It is almost impossible to turn back the clock. The fine line between reactive and active disengagement can be crossed overnight – that's when the infection begins to creep.

Remember, disengagement occurs when the employee, consciously or not, decides that he wants another job. He may not know where he's going to find it, but the minute the emotional break happens, disengagement starts.

If a manager understands the phases of disengagement and recognizes the symptoms and timeline, steps can be taken to prevent and/or reverse disengagement. As a manager, you should continually assess everyone who reports to you and determine where each employee fits within the phases.

The results produced by addressing disengagement symptoms can be both satisfying and impressive.

Mark was an executive secretary of an international human resources consulting company's New York office. Mark had long been frustrated by what he perceived as arbitrary policies and cutthroat politics, but he limited his disengagement to gossip and a generous helping of "sick days." One of Mark's biggest peeves was that his boss, the general manager, refused to let employees leave a few hours early before Thanksgiving or Christmas without first getting permission from corporate headquarters. Headquarters usually gave permission to leave early – until one particular Thanksgiving.

On that particular morning, Mark intercepted a fax from headquarters that the New York office was not to close early. In a fit of anger, Mark instantly moved from reactive to active disengagement. He shredded the fax in front of a co-worker, and then informed his boss that 2 p.m. was closing time. Needless to say the corporate president was perturbed when he called the office and discovered everyone had gone home early.

When Marks's actions were uncovered, not only was he fired, but headquarters also forced the New York office to remain open until 5 p.m. on Christmas Eve to compensate for the "stolen" time.

Everyone had known Mark was unhappy, but nothing had been done. The result was as predictable as the tides, yet ignored until the damage had already been done.

WATCH WHERE YOU PAY ATTENTION

Obviously, not every employee becomes disengaged. But every new employee does enjoy a "honeymoon" with those adrenaline-filled days. Managers, co-workers and reports pay more attention to new workers than they do seasoned ones. Problems begin when the honeymoon ends and the same people who lavished attention on the new recruit begin to take him for granted – unless he is a mediocre performer.

EXPECTING FISH TO FLY AND BIRDS TO SWIM

As a rule, managers devote excessive time to mediocre and poor performers, hoping against hope that the "fish can fly and birds can swim." Productive employees are often left to languish, saddled with extra responsibilities and tasks because they'll get the job done! It's a manager's unintentional punishment. Suddenly the top performers get more work and less attention. Meanwhile, mediocre workers are "rewarded" with more attention and lower expectations. The result? Productive workers feel unappreciated, underpaid and overworked – the perfect recipe for reactive disengagement.

In the TKG survey of more than 1,400 employees, 23% cited that excessive workloads had the most negative impact on their drive to do their best.

Many companies create incentive programs to boost mediocre performers' productivity. This is ridiculous! Ask yourself this question: "Do you truly believe that an employee actually thinks, 'I know how to perform better, but I won't unless I receive more incentives?'" Be realistic. Why should mediocre performers do better just because of an incentive? And, how long will it last if they do? Is doing better a matter of choice? Mentally healthy adults will always strive to do better. Who strives to do poorly?

Unfortunately, when a manager becomes aware of poor performance, she usually waits too long to speak with the individual, hoping the negative behavior will fix itself. Therein lies the biggest problem: **It's not about healing the virus of disengagement; it's about preventing it and eventually eliminating it.**

A WAKE-UP CALL

Did you know that poor performance by co-workers is one of the top reasons engaged employees leave their jobs? That's a wake-up call for managers if anything is.

92% of employees in a TKG survey agreed that their companies fail to identify or deal with poor performers.

ISOLATING THE VIRUS OF DISENGAGEMENT

At one time or another, many of us have experienced a workplace metamorphosis: from happy and engaged to sullen and enraged. The following case history involves some of the most common reasons for disengagement and reveals how many employees cycle through the "five phases" – from engagement to disengagement.

THE BOOK ON JAMES

James, a 35-year-old word processor, joined a Wall Street law firm in the spring of 1996. Although he was an aspiring playwright, James understood the odds of making a fortune on Broadway were very slim. For that reason, he decided to obtain the skills to become a legal secretary. The managing partner offered competitive salaries, as well as ample health, retirement and vacation benefits.

James enjoyed a typical "honeymoon" and an extended period of engagement, during which he acquired valuable and specialized skills that earned him raises. Despite several hardware and software upgrades,

James always mastered the requirements. In fact, he became more knowledgeable about certain processes and procedures than some of the attorneys. On the downside, the pace could become extremely frantic as deadline approached, and James was asked to work well into the night.

By the third year, the realities of the job and James' perceptions about the company had changed for the worse. Without soliciting input from employees, management decided that overtime would become mandatory. Initially, James would be asked in advance if he was available to stay late. Now, he was given no choice; work overtime or else. In addition, the workload had reached staggering proportions. New hires found they couldn't keep up with the pace and quit in a few months. Veteran legal secretaries had problems adjusting to new technology and were enrolled in training seminars and classes. Not James. He was "ol' reliable." On more than one occasion, the managing partner marveled that James was performing the work of three legal secretaries.

Gradually, colleagues began to notice changes in James' attitude. He had become sullen, angry and frequently whispered about the huge sums of money the partner was spending on new cars, safaris or the real estate he had just purchased. His grumbling began to infect co-workers, who also began venting against the managing partner and the office manager to whom they directly reported.

Although James cycled into Phase 3, it went unnoticed by management until he began acting in frustration. Because of all the mandatory overtime, James believed he had no time to spend with family and friends, much less time to pursue his vocation of playwriting. In response to the long hours and increased pressures, he began making angry comments whenever he was asked to work late. Only when James began behaving rudely to clients did management take notice. By this point, it was too late.

Even though the office manager and managing partner offered to adopt some of James' suggestions during Phase 3, James was already a lost cause. Burned out, frustrated and completely disengaged, James up and left the firm without even bothering to secure another position.

There are many morals to this story – some of which speak to preventing disengagement before it occurs. Others provide clues about how management can turn back the clock on disengagement by assessing current employees to determine levels of job satisfaction, feedback on management policies and behaviors, recommendations on process improvements, and most importantly, a feeling that management is listening to employees.

SPOTTING MENTAL ABSENCE

There are many underlying personal and work factors that must exist for the disengagement virus to grow and spread. Chiefly disengagement has become a coping mechanism for job-related stress, which often results from several factors:

○ People mismatched to positions

○ Little or no control over work patterns

○ Work pattern and behavior differences with boss

○ No involvement in decisions or changes

○ Lack of accountability

○ Lack of pride in the job one does

○ No recognition

○ Little or no opportunity to grow, learn, develop or contribute

○ Lack of future opportunities

○ Ineffective communication

By being alert to the early signs of disengagement, you have the opportunity to take steps to defuse the situation.

STEPS FOR DEFUSING THE DISENGAGEMENT PROCESS

1. Take the temperature of your organization often. Use unbiased tools and assessments to unearth the truth.

2. Continually coach employees to improve job performance.

3. Alert employees when they're about to make a mistake.

4. Teach employees new ideas and concepts so they can increase their value.

5. Be brave enough to communicate in clear, direct language.

6. Focus on the individual's assets.

7. Be honest in understanding your own strengths and limitations as a leader.

8. Pay attention to your "quiet talent," recognizing their consistency and dedication; reward them in quiet ways.

9. Invite top performers to meetings they would not normally attend.

It is critical that managers know their employees' job satisfaction status. If disengagement has set in, a thorough assessment must be completed before any solutions are prescribed. Managers need to uncover the roots of disengagement and define the focus of improvement. Trying to determine reasons for disengagement by simply asking the employee is like trying to diagnose a heart condition by merely listening to the heart. And, the employee must agree that your assessments and analyses are correct. Opinions play no role in diagnosing disengagement.

6

FIRING IS A FAVOR

The damage that an unproductive and disengaged worker can cause is impossible to tally.

In my research on organizational patterns, I have found that coworkers recognize disengagement much sooner than management. As a result, the impact on employee morale, as well as its effect on customers and productivity, is often devastating. Dissatisfaction, frustration and constant griping create a vortex that sucks the enthusiasm out of even the most productive and engaged workers.

We have recognized that it takes the typical manager nine months before recognizing unacceptable work patterns. Then, the manager lingers another three months before addressing the issue. This allows the employee to remain actively disengaged for 12 whole months – one full year! Even worse, after trying to address the performance problems with the disengaged individual, it takes the manager an additional six to nine months before he's willing to fire the employee. This is especially damaging considering that many company policies state that before an employee is "separated," he must be put on a three-month "PIP" (Performance Improvement Plan). If the employee agrees to be placed in a PIP – and most do to buy time – he must show improvement by meeting set goals and demonstrating a renewed commitment to the job and the company. If he does not meet requirements after three months, he can be fired.

While this sounds reasonable, consider this: If the employee continues to be disengaged, his disengagement period now totals 16 to 21 months, a period during which he has continued to negatively affect other employees and customers. This pattern exists at all levels – from frontline employees to executives.

Sixty-eight percent of an employee's productivity is directly attributable to the supervisor.

If you make the wrong decision in hiring, recognize it early and deal with it. Either change the position or change the person. "Fixing" people can actually yield negative returns in productivity. You need to know when not to retain an employee and why.

A best friend, Bob Lapidus – founder and former CEO of Bob's Stores – was a retail genius. Bob's approach to people was simple, yet powerful: Recognize them when they do well, and let them go quickly when they don't.

So, when is it time to fire? When you first think about it! Don't ponder it; don't postpone it. Just recognize that you've made a hiring mistake, then fix it. In the long run, it's doing as much of a favor for the wrong-fit employee as it is for you.

A good example of "firing as a favor" comes from my experience as a general merchandise manager. I had a sportswear buyer who was dedicated, hardworking, loyal, professional and a good listener. However, she lacked enthusiasm, the "gift of gab" and negotiating skills. In the days of the "garmento" mentality — slap them on the back, you're my best friend — vendors did not accept her. They complained that she was too quiet, standoffish and gave no feedback.

In hindsight, she was a gem! But in those days, understanding employee behavior wasn't at the top of my to-do list. Repeated attempts at changing her behavior proved fruitless, so I "accepted her resignation." Days later she found a position at a company whose behaviors and values matched her own. She became a satisfied, happy and successful long-term employee.

Since then, when we talk, she has repeatedly told me that the best thing I ever did was to convince her to leave. She would never have made that decision on her own because it went against her behavior preferences. She disliked change, avoided confrontation, was not a risk taker, and was very loyal. Miserable as she was, she would have never, ever quit on her own.

FEARLESS FIRING

Remember, by the time you realize that you need to fire an employee, you also realize that it is truly a favor for you and for them. So, the best thing to do is to make it as fast and simple as possible.

Q: What is the best way for a manager to fire an employee?
A: *Fast. "Joe, you and I know that this job is not right for you. I don't want to see you unhappy..."*

Q: What is the worst way to fire someone?
A: *Review everything that the person did wrong. Or even worse, review everything he did well, but explain that it's just not working out lately.*

Q: What is the most common way to fire?

A: *Blaming everything from poor revenues to company cutbacks to reduction of responsibilities on this person – everything but the real reason.*

Do the individual a favor. Show them how to face the fact that the match is simply not there.

Do other employees a favor. They usually know before you that a co-worker is ineffective or a detriment to the company.

Do yourself a favor. How much time are you spending with the poor performer? Your time is costly to you and your company. Make better use of your time by developing engaged employees with potential.

Do your customers a favor. An unhappy worker does not deliver satisfying and happy service.

SHE CAN, BUT WILL SHE?
SKILL VS. WILL

S kill and will – the best employees have both. What's the
difference? One can be taught, the other can't. Confusing
the two can cause turnover and disengagement.

Skills can be learned, adapted, changed and improved. Will is an
internal drive mechanism bolted together from values, convictions
rewards, dreams and disappointments. Will is an engine fueled by
beliefs that define behavior. Will is not about whether you can do
the job, but whether you will. What you believe is what you think,
and what you think determines how you act.

*Debra, a salesperson, secretly believes that customers do not want to be
"bothered." After all, she hates to be bothered when she shops. However,
she has been trained to approach customers or risk reprimands from her
manager. So when the manager is on the floor, Debra asks customers*

how she can help. When he's not, she doesn't. Debra even admitted telling customers that she doesn't want to approach them, but has to. She says to customers, "I'm sure you don't want me buggin' you, and I won't. It's just that they told me I have to come over and talk to you — so I am." She thinks, if a customer needs me, she'll let me know. Why doesn't Debra consistently approach customers? She believes she is right and the manager is wrong, and based on that belief, she chooses to behave in a way that is not in compliance with the standards. Debra may have the skill, but not the will.

Measuring ability is a surface assessment. You may gauge the level of skill, but not the will. Observe waiters in a restaurant. Many are skilled; some of them could care less if your water glass is empty. It seems the latter are "waiters" because they're waiting for a movie producer to discover them.

Assessing behavior goes one step further. You can determine if an employee or prospective employee will display a natural behavior through behavior testing. But conscious behavior accounts for only 50% of the actions that a person will take in any given situation.

This means that half the time, when an employee interacts with a customer, she may rely on a core belief that results in inappropriate behavior, like Debra who did not want to bother customers.

Training is not the remedy for this problem. The final assessment in hiring and evaluating ongoing performance requires you to take not only an inventory of an employee's or applicant's behaviors, but also of their beliefs and values.

Another salesperson, John, sold fashion apparel. His productivity was below average and had not improved during his probation period.

Termination was imminent. John was a nice guy and a good employee, but he was costing the company money.

John's short, stocky stature made him uncomfortable selling apparel to people he perceived as more attractive and stylish. He felt awkward recommending styles and colors. John's position also required a great deal of details and facts about product knowledge.

John completed a behavior and values assessment. It showed that he was enthusiastic, people oriented, persuasive and wanted to work in an autonomous, creative atmosphere. In terms of the behavior needed for the job, John was well suited. However, the key problem was his belief that he was somehow "inferior" to his customers.

The recommendation from the assessment results was to transfer John to the card and gift department. Management was skeptical. How could John "earn his keep" working in cards and gifts without a salary reduction? Reluctantly, management agreed. Result? John blossomed.

Within 30 days, he was generating three times his previous sales by selling cards! He was actively engaged in his job. Within three months, he had created a unique business. He used his enthusiasm and natural persuasive behavior to convince customers that he could save them time if they let him do the card and gift shopping for them. He developed an impressive client file system where he documented special occasions whenever a customer was purchasing cards. John would select appropriate cards a week before the occasion and send them to his customers with a note that any unused items could be returned. He also sent fun little gifts – like mugs and trinkets – suitable to the occasion. During his first year, John's sales of $362,000 earned him a top award. By the way, John never had any returns from his customers – not a one!

THE DEFINING DIFFERENCE – YOUR BELIEFS AND VALUES

Beliefs and values dictate how people interact with the world. When an individual's values are aligned with the values important to the job and recognized and rewarded by the organization, the outcome is engagement and high performance. Beliefs and values cannot be imposed. They are fundamental human qualities that are as individual as fingerprints. Only when you have defined them can you align your people with positions at which they'll shine.

SELF-SABOTAGING BELIEFS

Many managers shrink discussions about beliefs, values, behaviors and human nature and retreat to the safety of training programs. Beliefs and values do change, but not through training. They change based on the individual's human issues and experiences.

In another TKG survey of more than 800 managers, covering 27 belief categories, eight common self-sabotaging beliefs were discovered:

1. I just don't have time to deal with all of the "soft stuff" (people issues).

2. Turnover won't stop. People don't take their jobs seriously. Why should I invest time and money on people who will leave anyway?

3. The more I compliment them (employees), the more money they want.

4. I don't mind answering employees' questions, but some of them are really stupid.

5. I don't have time to listen to people who take forever to make a point.

6. I don't understand this company. How can I keep my credibility as a manager and carry out policies I don't agree with?

7. The business is a struggle. No matter what you do, someone will find a reason to change it, so why bother being creative? Just follow the rules.

8. I know what's best – if only "my people" would listen to me.

When beliefs like these exist, they propagate the virus of disengagement. Values and beliefs cannot be ignored. As you evaluate your employees' satisfaction status, it is important to include an assessment of their beliefs and values. What is important to them? What do they hold in high regard? What principles and practices do they live by at work? The answers to these questions will help you find out what influences how they behave at work.

8

BEING A FIT FOR THE JOB –
WHY WHALES DON'T WALK

Ask yourself, "How much expense and aggravation could I save by matching people with jobs that fit naturally? How much job satisfaction, productivity and customer satisfaction could we gain?"

Every job applicant is unique, and every company's culture is distinct and unique as well. Therefore, every company should have a job template, an employee profile and a method for determining if the employee is a match for the job.

When you hire a person for a job that matches his natural behavior, several things happen: The person enjoys doing the job and instinctively focuses on completing the job. When the behavior required for a job does not match the natural behavior of the employee, the person expends a great deal of energy trying to adjust his behavior to fit the needs of the job.

A poor job fit requires the employee to operate on a battery pack that needs constant recharging, but a good job fit gives you an employee who is always "plugged in" – receiving continuous energy flow. The stress of "charging up" unnatural behaviors results in behavioral problems, illness or drug/alcohol abuse, all of which increase benefit costs and absenteeism, while simultaneously decreasing their quality of work and productivity.

ASSESSING INDIVIDUAL BEHAVIOR

Stephen Covey wrote in his book, *Principle-Centered Leadership*, "In a very real sense, there is no such thing as organizational behavior, there is only individual behavior."

So how well do you really understand the individual behavior of your direct reports? How do you approach the people you must encourage, develop, coach and keep engaged? As human beings, we cannot avoid bringing personal biases, opinions and preferences into the workplace. We make comparisons and judgments based on our own values, beliefs and behaviors.

Assessments often reveal marked differences between what a manager *thinks is true* versus *what is actually true*. Managers who rely on validated assessments are better able to retain engaged talent at far higher percentages than managers who rely solely on their instincts.

For years, I have successfully used a survey process in hundreds of companies – one that identifies the critical factors that contribute to superior job performance. The key to individual performance excellence lies in the combination of behaviors, values and personal attributes. This assessment provides a clear reading on how employees do what they do, why they do what they do, and whether they will do what they say they will do.

Each individual has a unique way of working. Each individual, placed in the right job with the right guidance, possesses incredible potential. But each person may not want to be a hard-driving, winner-takes-all player. There are many workers who are consistent, loyal and quietly productive. Unfortunately, these employees are often overlooked for promotions and critical projects. Managers who expect and prefer assertive, outgoing or energetic people rarely select those supportive doers as team leaders. This is wrong and unfair. It's also limiting for the team and the organization.

ENSURING ENGAGEMENT

Three construction workers are taking their lunch breaks high over the city. "What have you got, Joe?" one asks. "Tuna," says Joe. "How about you?" "Turkey," answers the second guy, who asks the third, "What about you, Nick?" "Baloney," Nick answers. "I hate baloney. If I get baloney one more time, I'm going to jump off this building." The next day, they asked each other again. Nick opens his lunch box, unwraps his sandwich and screams, "BALONEY AGAIN!" He jumps off the building. The other two workers watch him plummet to the pavement. "Shame," says the first one. "Yeah," agrees the second. "But the real shame is that he packs his own lunch."

When you make a hiring decision, you are in essence packing your own lunch. Although managers claim they hate the baloney of turnover and low productivity, they continually serve it to themselves because they fail to ensure employee engagement up-front.

Employee disengagement and turnover are the inevitable results of mismatching people to jobs, people to companies and people to people. For workers to be productive, they must believe in themselves and their contributions. They must also believe that their talents and personalities are compatible with the requirements of the job, and that they fit well with their co-workers.

Basic skills were sufficient criteria in the age of the assembly line. But any job where interactive skills are a factor requires precise matching of individual styles to the jobs, company, co-workers and customers.

Before you can match a person to a job, however, you must be clear on what you're matching. The organization and its people, the culture and customers and an accurate profile for each position should be clearly defined before the interviewing and hiring processes begin. When the position profile truly describes the attributes most needed for superior performance, it becomes easier to determine whether the individual you are interviewing truly fits the job.

Preventing disengagement is a process that begins before the applicant is hired. It starts when you match the right people with the right positions, and it continues when you put the focus on people.

Dave was hired as an executive trainee by a Midwestern retailer. The company invested five years in training and developing Dave, eventually promoting him to store manager for a $90 million operation. Within three months, Dave developed a series of health problems. He took more sick days in six months than in his entire career with the company. Store sales dropped significantly as did Dave's productivity. Management was stunned. How could a person change so dramatically?

Although the dilemma was clear, the next steps were not. I recommended a total assessment of Dave's behavior preferences, values, beliefs and job attributes which showed that Dave was quality-oriented, very systematic in his approach to work and procedures. Naturally patient, with good listening skills, he required a paced environment in which work was completed with emphasis on quality and process. His current work environment was not in line with his natural abilities and needs. Instead, all of the focus was on just-doing-it-to-get-it-done.

A recommendation to transfer Dave to a smaller suburban store with fewer employees was presented, and the move was made. Within one year, Dave's results surprised both management and Dave himself. No sick days, reduced employee turnover and a 22% increase in store sales.

DISCOVER THE D & A

For effective recruiting, hiring, retention and employee engagement, it is important to have four specific areas. I call this the DEFINE & ALIGN (D & A) process, and it begins with answering questions in these four areas:

1. SELF: Who am I? What do I value? How do I interact with others?

2. JOB: What are the success requirements for this position?

3. ORGANIZATION: What do we believe? What do we value? How do we behave?

4. EMPLOYEE / APPLICANT: What are the natural abilities of this person? What does he/she value and believe? What behaviors do these beliefs generate? How will he/she go about doing the job?

These four definitions are developed using assessment tools that profile individuals (applicants and employees), the job and the company. When the profiling process is complete (DEFINE), the result is a clear definition of the right employee for the employer, the job and the organization. The "right job" definition then serves as a template.

It helps you (ALIGN) look for a person with sharply defined common contours that precisely fit the job requirements.

The D & A process is almost as simple as determining whether Mozart would make a good musician. It's about determining attributes, natural abilities, attitudes, inclinations, motivators, etc., and creating a natural fit into a job that calls for those attributes.

WHY THE D & A PROCESS IS WORTH YOUR TIME

It's tempting to skip the Self and Organization profiling and immediately delve into the Job/Applicant/Employee definitions and alignment. This is not a good idea. Organizations and managers each have distinct profiles.

Let's say you have a close fit between the job and the applicant, but you have failed to include profiling Self and the Organization. You risk encountering the top two reasons why so many good people leave – continuous conflict with the corporate culture or conflict with a boss with whom they can't get in sync. So, do yourself a favor. Define all four of the D & A profiles:

1. **Self Definition:** As a manager or employer, what is your management behavior? Do you prefer to work through people or with people? What is your communication style? Are you task- or idea-oriented? Knowing how you communicate, manage and lead allows you to recognize, understand and adapt to other behavioral styles.

2. **Job Definition:** Many employers expect employees to fit a job that is too loosely defined, if it is defined at all. An example: "Your job is to sell to and service customers so they are satisfied." Too much is assumed and too little is communicated in this

job statement. Ask instead: "If this job could talk, what would it say?" For example:

- This job requires and consists of many changes.

- In this job, you will have to carry out unpopular decisions and policies.

- The job requires employees to persist steadily at routine work.

- This job requires the ability to manage diverse types of people.

- This job requires an ability to follow detailed instruction with patience.

- The job requires commitment to stay at this job level for an indefinite period of time.

In job profiling, job attributes like these are rated by assigning a value of 1 to 4 to each statement, where 1 means most important to the job and 4 means least important. Then the job profile is compared to the applicant or employee's profile to gauge compatibility.

A job should be defined from several sources, and differences should be reconciled before the profile/template is used to recruit, hire or promote. Once ratified, the profile serves as common ground for evaluating applicants.

3. **Organization Definition:** What defines this company's culture? How does the company deal with problems and challenges? Is it aggressive? Cutting edge? How does the company relate to employees? To customers? Is there a high task or a high idea

emphasis? How are rules and protocols handled? Does the status quo rule the day, or does the company value innovation?

The assessments used here focus on how management behaves day-to-day rather than relying on some "corporate vision" statement that may have lost its meaning long ago.

Successful companies are realistic in assessing what they are and how they act. They are vocal about what works and what doesn't. When companies face the fact that there are no "ideals," they can go about determining what their unique values, beliefs and behaviors say about them. Then the choice becomes simple. We like who we are and let's continue, or this is not what we're about: Let's change. No amount of discussion gets to the root of these issues like a well-designed, unbiased assessment tool.

4. **Applicant/Employee Definition:** How can employers gain insight into job applicants beyond the resume and interview? Employers must understand individual preferences – personal "drivers" that go beyond what interviewers perceive. Human bias is removed by assessing communication styles, behavior preferences, beliefs, values and job attributes. These assessments also answer questions such as: What must this applicant learn? What tools does this person need to be self-motivated and productive? Does the person see the job correctly? An assessment that goes beyond evaluating words, actions or surface behaviors will reveal the right hiring decision or transform current employees into more productive team members.

The "graphs" and "wheels" and ratings in respondents' results produced by these assessments allow companies to see where differences exist –

the gulfs between how jobs are described vs. the day-to-day reality; how managers view themselves vs. how direct reports view them; how the company actually behaves toward its people vs. how the company believes it behaves.

You can view a sample of these assessments at **www.kabachnick.com.**

ELEMENTS OF CONTROL
ENCOURAGE ENGAGEMENT

Two guys are riding a bicycle built for two. They come to a steep hill. The guy in front says, "We're really going to have to work hard to get up this hill," and he starts pedaling for all he's worth. He pedals until he thinks he's going to pass out. Finally, they get to the top, and the front guy turns and says, "Man, I thought we'd never make it." "Me neither," says the guy in back. "If I hadn't kept the brake on, we'd have rolled back for sure."

DEFINE EXPECTATIONS

How many people in your organization are pedaling for all they're worth, and how many are pushing down on the brakes – both feeling they are doing the right thing? People are motivated when they understand and agree with what is expected of them. Strong definitions create expectations, and clearly understood expectations clarify communications, which help to improve self-esteem. Employees with high self-esteem participate. The key to long-term productivity is participation.

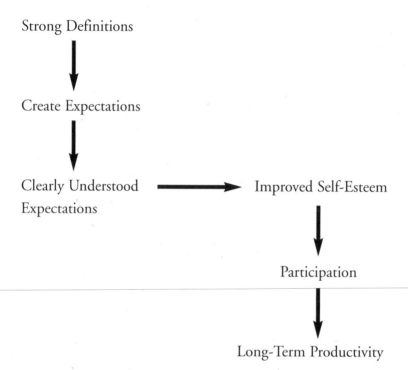

Clearly Defined Expectations Encourage Long-Term Productivity.

Then, of course, there are job descriptions, which are typically a list of job-specific tasks. Hiring managers review these documents with applicants during the interview and then present them, as a reminder of responsibilities – everyday job tasks – once the person is hired. What happens to these documents?

A challenge: Ask any one of your employees for their job description. Can she recite it? Does she remember it? Does she know where she even put it? So much for job responsibilities!

What about accountabilities? In organizations worldwide, there is a common pattern. Most companies do not differentiate between responsibilities – the tasks and accountabilities – the output or desired results of completing the job tasks. Yet, there is a big difference between the two, and it has a major impact on employee engagement and customer satisfaction.

At a steel cable company, the receptionist has the first-level customer service position. Most of the calls she receives are from the company's clients. I asked her, "For what are you primarily responsible?" She responds, "Answering the phones." I then asked, "What are you accountable for?" Her response was a blank stare. It was apparent that she had no understanding that her accountability went way beyond her responsibility to answer the phone. She was accountable for ensuring that at the end of the phone call, the customer had a positive feeling and felt satisfied about his brief experience with the company.

Granted, the receptionist's position is a basic level of employment. But, this response does not change as employees move up in the organization. Managers do not know that they are accountable for talent retention and employee development. Their job descriptions don't typically say that. Go all the way to the top and look at recent corporate scandals where the CEOs and other top executives claimed they didn't know about accounting infractions. Well, who was accountable? Being accountable means thinking beyond responsibility and thinking about the outcomes that result long after the task is done well.

P.A.L.

Here is an alternative method of managing that encourages participation, eliminates baby-sitting and stresses accountability. I call this our **P.A.L.** – *Personal Accountability List.* Ask an employee to write down what he thinks his job requires him to do (the tasks) and how he needs to do the job (the behaviors). These are the responsibilities. Our research shows that desired job behaviors usually vary based on employees' perceptions of the job.

Then ask him to write down what he believes are the chief reasons why he needs to perform these tasks and exhibit the behaviors, and how this will affect customers and company goals. These are the accountabilities.

An example of responsibilities for a customer service representative in ABC Company would be:

- Acknowledge customers quickly.
- Greet them politely.
- Solve problems efficiently and respectfully.

The job would require the following behaviors:

- Ability to listen
- Questioning skills
- Flexibility
- Adaptability
- Problem solving

Examples of accountabilities for the customer service representative might be to ensure customer satisfaction and high ratings on customer service scores.

Responsibilities for a manager's position might include:

- ○ Evaluate business results and performance on a daily, weekly and monthly basis.

- ○ Ensure all aspects of operations are running efficiently and effectively to manage expenses.

- ○ Conduct regularly scheduled information meetings with employees.

- ○ Meet with each employee monthly to determine performance and satisfaction levels and address individual needs.

Required behaviors:

- ○ Self management

- ○ Setting priorities

- ○ Driving for goal achievement

- ○ Effective communication

A manager's accountabilities would be to build a high-performance team and achieve business results (sales and profits).

USING THE P.A.L.

Provide adequate time for employees to complete this exercise. Then follow up with a discussion about their individual P.A.L. If tasks or behaviors have been omitted, ask about the omissions and discuss. Focus on the *results* instead of the process.

Then, you need to gain agreement and commitment from the employee. You do this by asking a simple question: "Jim, do you believe your P.A.L. is a good description of your responsibilities and accountabilities and what you need to accomplish in your job?" More than likely, the answer will be yes. Next, the critical question: "Jim, will you commit to do what you have listed?" Again, the answer is usually yes. Now ask the employee to sign what he has written. Meanwhile, make the commitment to help Jim whenever he needs guidance. If the employee does not measure up to these expectations, show him the "contract" and ask: "Jim, why aren't you doing what you promised?" A P.A.L. and gaining agreement to the list are powerful tools that you can deploy when an employee is not meeting expectations and needs to be reminded of his responsibilities and accountabilities.

With a written job P.A.L. commitment, you eliminate the need for "to-do" lists, daily verbal instructions, constant reminders of basic tasks and management baby-sitting. By having employees define their jobs in their own words, you determine their understanding of the job requirements and accountabilities. At the same time, employees feel a sense of control and commitment because it's now up to them to do what must be done.

UNDERSTAND AND ALIGN PERSONAL GOALS

People work for different reasons. Some work primarily for personal identification and self-esteem. They are what they do. Others may work just to earn a livelihood. Overall, employees work for compensation, but are influenced to stay for other reasons such as respect and relationships. Compensation may be the most important factor, but other rewards run a close second. Chief among them is control. When employees believe they've lost control over their jobs – and therefore, a significant part of their lives – problems begin.

Control is defined by participation, which produces feelings of belonging, contribution and stability. It is as important to an organization's success as it is to an individual's success.

ASK YOURSELF: What are your personal goals?

ACCEPT: It is fine if work is of secondary importance. Something else like parenting or studying for a degree is more important.

DISCOVER: the passions that drive an employee's beliefs, which in turn drive behavior. Example: Linda's passion is to be a medical biologist in three years. Her belief: I will do a great job at work so that I can pay my tuition. Her behavior: commitment and dedication to doing an exemplary job.

Many employees are afraid to disclose their true goals and passions for fear they will be viewed as uncommitted. Are you forcing employees to pretend? Cut through this charade.

GIVE: specific goals and the freedom to achieve them in a personalized way.

DO NOT: place specific focus on how tasks are performed.

ASK: Is this employee producing the desired results?

Remember, this is about CONTROL. Control is the critical belief that drives behaviors. The belief that one has or does not have control over her life is the prime difference between an employee who will remain loyal and engaged over the long-term and one who will eventually move toward disengagement.

TKG research identified some common beliefs in many organizations:

○ Managers believe they must justify their positions and pay by controlling what people do, and when and how they do it.

○ Workers believe they have no control over their job and try to "steal" control whenever possible.

To steal control, employees may take a longer break or lunch hour, take an extra break, fail to perform necessary tasks when the boss is not around, call in sick or make false excuses for absenteeism, come in late and spread false rumors.

Everyone has priorities, passions and goals that take precedence over work. Many times, they are not life-and-death matters, but simply personal priorities. What are your priorities? Do they always make sense to someone else? Probably not. But sometimes, your priorities reflect a need to regain your balance, recover your energy or exercise some control over your life. Individual passions and beliefs are your inner motivators.

My husband, Phil, follows the UConn Huskies (University of Connecticut) basketball team with ardor and passion. He'll do whatever is humanly possible to not miss a game. If he was working for you, and told you he couldn't stay late one evening because he wanted to attend a game, what would you do?

Your answer would depend on your beliefs about life and work balance, about control as an innate human need, and about re-energizing to increase productivity. As Phil's manager, you should know about his interest in UConn basketball and how much he values watching the games. Because you knew Phil, his beliefs, values and interests, and you had frequent conversations with him, you and Phil could plan for him to make as many games as possible. He would be more productive and more engaged because you had interest in him and what was important to him.

10

DEVOTED, DETERMINED, DISGUISED – DO YOU RECOGNIZE THEM?

Every organization today is searching for talent. Talent is exciting, energizing and enveloping. Talented people draw you in with their creativity and innovation. Their ideas and commitment to making something happen are infectious. Talent comes in many forms. Unfortunately, because of misperceptions many managers fail to see talent in its different disguises.

Highly talented people or "A" players are employees who are hungry for results, impatient for promotions, willing to sacrifice life for work and its meaning in helping them identify who they are as individuals.

Then there are the "B" players, also highly talented people, who are loyal, dedicated, focused on helping others succeed and prefer to give the spotlight to someone else. They are the "worker bees" who rarely, if ever, make personal demands. "B" players are not disengaged. "B" players are balanced – an enigma to "A" players, who truly do not understand them. As a result, "B" players and their values are frequently overlooked. Their contributions are too often minimized, and they can easily leave others confused. Hiring managers routinely pass on them, primarily because they perform so poorly in interviews. But remember, they don't like the spotlight. They are, however, the foundation of an organization's productivity. Highly developed listening skills naturally make them the sounding board for others' issues and concerns. As a result of their caring nature, they easily become the behind-the-scenes counselors and coaches. Many "B" players are mistaken as disengaged, most often the result of "A" players' perceptions.

Distinguishing characteristics for the "A" and "B" players:

"A" Players:	"B" Players:
Task-oriented	Relationship-oriented
Work to get it done	Work to get it done right
Want things to happen now	Enjoy seeing things happen
Set high goals and change them	Set achievable goals
Must win the game	Like playing the game
Need to lead	Like to follow
Approach aggressively	Approach cautiously

The significant difference between "B" players and disengaged workers is their heart. "B" players truly care about their company, co-workers and customers. They are mentally present – in contrast to disengaged workers who are more self-focused and mentally absent.

PART-TIMERS ARE NOT "COVERAGE"

According to the U.S. Bureau of Labor Statistics, many experts believe that within a few years the U.S. will have a shortfall of 10 million workers, mostly in the frontline service sector. It is predicted that it will be increasingly more difficult to find employees willing to work for minimum wage. The goods news is that there will be more and more part-time workers available – thanks to changing beliefs and values, work and job preferences, social needs and retirees who don't want to retire.

The biggest problem faced by this important group of workers is the attitudes of their bosses, managers and full-time workers who too often regard part-timers' contributions as insignificant.

TKG's research reveals that part-timers' performance scores are approximately 30% higher than full-timers'. They also show a higher energy level, do not get bored as easily, and are less likely to get caught up in workplace politics.

FULL-TIME APPRECIATION

To tap this resource and prevent disengagement among highly productive part-timers, you must view them as genuine contributors to the company. Then, consider these suggestions:

○ Review your company policies regarding part-timers' hiring practices, pay, benefits, schedules and other areas where you may be hanging on to "sacred cows."

○ Show respect for part-timers. They should not be relegated to positions that are unimportant and tasks that nobody wants.

○ Provide guidance and education. Do not exclude part-timers from training sessions and meetings. Encourage them and make it easy for them to participate in meetings. Offer ideas and recommendations. Give them an opportunity.

○ Acknowledge their temporary status. It's no secret that many part-timers will be with you temporarily. Bring this out in the open. Explain that while they may be with you for a brief time, you will provide them with opportunities to help them achieve their goals. All you ask in return is that they be responsible, attentive and give their best.

○ Partner a full-timer with a part-timer. Ask a full-timer to communicate news, important information, policy changes, meeting notes and general correspondence to the part-timer. Reward the full-timer for this responsibility.

○ Touch base regularly with your part-timers, at least once per month. Build a relationship. Find out how they are doing and offer feedback. The time you spend with part-timers will be noticed, and it will send the important message that you consider part-timers valuable workers.

○ Recognize and value seniors who work part time. Older employees bring vast experience with them. Many were managers and leaders in their pre-retirement days. Ask them to become mentors. Ask for their advice. Make them feel important. Everyone will benefit.

INVENTIVE INCENTIVES – THINK BEYOND MONEY

If "man does not live by bread alone," neither does he work for money alone. A tempting salary may lure hordes of eager applicants to your door, but it won't keep employees engaged and productive for very long. Employees sign on for the money, but they stay for non-monetary benefits, including opportunities for personal and professional development.

Salary raises and cash bonuses do not make for good incentive programs. In fact, they frequently backfire. If you have ever felt like the more cash you give, the less satisfied your employees are, you're not alone. Cold, hard cash leaves some employees, well, cold. Worse yet, financial incentives may actually send the wrong message, rewarding mediocre employees for behaviors and performance levels they should have displayed all along.

By contrast, recognition programs that offer workers non-monetary incentives – or combinations of cash and other tangible rewards – create lasting and memorable experiences that leave employees feeling fully appreciated.

WHERE "BRIBES" FAIL, RECOGNITION RULES

As heads of a national consulting company, Bob Romano and Barbara Sanfillippo have conducted hundreds of culture climate surveys. Their studies consistently find that the top two reasons for employee disengagement are 1) lack of recognition and appreciation; and 2) lack of communication. Their surveys also reveal that employees participating in cash incentive programs without a strong recognition are less motivated and less satisfied than those who are made to feel appreciated through a pure recognition program.

Pure recognition – an acknowledgement (by word or deed) that "shows genuine appreciation for a specific behavior."

"People like money, but they still need to feel appreciated," explains Romano. "It's like the parents who don't spend time with their children and think they can buy their love with lavish gifts. The kids know better and the employees do, too."

Unlike merchandise and travel, cash awards create little emotional value or memories that motivate long after the cash is spent. Recognizing top performers in front of their peers is a proven method of recognition that makes an indelible impression on the psyche of most people and motivates a lot longer than cash. Today's employees may feel guilty spending cash on a nice dinner or weekend trip, but when you offer them a memorable experience, it creates goodwill toward your company.

"If you give me the money, I might feel guilty using it for an incredible experience," says Sanfillipo. "When you give me an awesome experience, I feel good about the company. It allows me to do something in my life I wouldn't normally do."

I don't suggest that you substitute theatre tickets, spa treatments and employee-of-the-month plaques for competitive salaries and benefits packages. And I certainly don't recommend that you entirely eliminate cash bonuses or pay raises as part of your incentive strategy. All employees want to feel valued, and a good wage, health benefits, end-of-year bonuses, etc., are basic tools for motivating and demonstrating your appreciation. But when you move beyond the basics – when you want workers to go above and beyond – when you want active engagement – non-monetary incentives often prove more effective than cash.

A few final words on inventive incentives: It's important to determine what types of incentives your employees would consider meaningful and valuable. Limit their debates and votes to comparisons of various non-monetary options. In other words, don't ask workers to choose between cash or prizes. Invariably, most workers will choose the money. Your goal is to design memorable incentives that employees will associate with their exceptional performance and reward them for remaining engaged.

PREVENT AND PRESERVE - MORE DISENGAGEMENT VACCINES

T he best antidote for avoiding the disengagement virus is to find various ways of keeping your employees engaged.

Here are **five effective strategies** to consider:

STRATEGY ONE - INTERNAL MENTORING PROGRAMS
When employees have the freedom to consult someone other than their boss for guidance, problem solving, conflict resolution and other issues, they are less stressed, more comfortable taking action and resolve issues faster. For one thing, the boss is often the cause of these issues. If unresolved, these issues can fester and lead to disengagement.

A successful mentoring program is a formal structured process taught to both mentor and the mentored. Mentoring begins by matching mentors with "mentees" or "pupils" according to shared beliefs, behaviors and values. Both mentor and mentee complete an assessment that assures the match is right. When done correctly, mentoring programs usually require four to six hours a month and last for about a year.

Employees view the program as an employment benefit, and few managers would disagree. Many executives claim they would never have reached their level of success without a mentor. Here are a few benefits that senior management attributes to formal mentoring:

- Promotes employee retention, higher productivity and improved morale.

- Executives make better hiring choices, thanks to a larger in-house talent pool.

- Employees require less time to be "brought up to speed" in new positions.

- Prevents good employees from falling off the fast track.

Because of these benefits, mentoring absolutely helps to ensure engagement.

STRATEGY TWO – ONE-ON-ONE EXECUTIVE COACHING

Have you ever started an exercise program? How long did your commitment last? Was sticking with the program more difficult than the actual exercises? If so, you're not alone, and this explains why so much exercise equipment gathers cobwebs in the darkest corners of garages.

But what if a personal trainer had worked with you – someone to guide you through the routines and keep you motivated? Would that have encouraged you to stick with the program? After all, when you sign with a personal trainer, you have an obligation to make your appointments, and most people hate to disappoint the instructor.

An executive coach is like a personal trainer. His first step is to identify an executive's needs and limitations, as well as her barriers to success as a leader. This process incorporates various assessment tools that supply objective, unbiased information that override opinions, perceptions and hearsay.

The executive completes several assessments prior to the first session with the coach. Both review the assessment results and outline her development needs. In my years as a coach and confidant to leaders worldwide, I have found the following attributes to be the most lacking when creating an individual development plan:

- ○ Self management
- ○ Conflict resolution
- ○ Decision making
- ○ Delegation
- ○ Objective listening
- ○ Image and personal style
- ○ Building effective work groups
- ○ Creating, defining and communicating goals and personal vision
- ○ Presentation skills

The coach's purpose is to act as a sounding board and mirror, allowing the executive to clearly see the impact of her behavior. Coaching is part training, part analysis, part feedback and part conflict resolution.

Coaching is often employed as an intervention tool to prevent executives from leaving and an important part of succession planning. Companies recognize that, in many cases, the lack of one or two skills keep the executive from becoming a top performer. Unfortunately, the executive is usually the last to identify her own weaknesses. This awareness gap can frustrate the executive. She becomes disengaged and then looks for employment elsewhere.

When the average company addresses an executive's limitations, the person is usually asked to attend seminars or workshops. Our research shows that – aside from learning basic management skills – seminars produce few, if any, lasting results. Few executives are willing to discuss limitations in front of a peer group, so their individual needs are not met. Executives don't implement the recommendations because there is no follow-up or accountability.

Coaching is necessary for anyone who wants to achieve higher levels of productivity.

STRATEGY THREE – BUILD A BETTER TEAM

As a concept, teamwork is often overrated and poorly defined. Many managers and executives use the term "teamwork" as their pie-in-the-sky panacea for all employee problems. I've heard, "Jill's not a team player; that's the problem," or "My people need to work as a team." On one occasion, an executive challenged me to "build a solid team." I discovered that the real problem was poorly defined responsibilities and a lack of results-oriented focus. In the end, I determined that conflict management was the missing ingredient, not teamwork.

The word "teamwork" means so many different things to so many people. When I'm asked to help people work better as a team, I start by asking, "What kind of team do you want? Is it like a baseball team where everyone has a specific and stationary position (a shortstop isn't supposed to chase balls hit into the left field corner), or like a football team, where everyone is in constant motion. (Whether you're an end or a linebacker, if the ball comes your way, grab it and run)."

I often hear managers say, "My people are always arguing; no one gets along; they don't know how to work together." To which I reply, "Is it really teamwork we're talking about or is it about conflict resolution?" Inevitably, it's not about teamwork. It's more about the conflicts that arise when people don't understand each other's work preferences and communication styles. When people understand their co-workers and learn to adapt – lo and behold, they begin to work well together.

An effective team-building program encourages individuals to understand and appreciate diversity. Team members learn about differences in communication, thinking and problem-solving styles. Using results from an assessment, team members learn about their own preferences before learning how to understand others. The different work styles can be classified in this way:

○ Implementer: Creative

○ Conductor: Competitive, direct, change agent

○ Persuader: Process-oriented, independent, optimistic

○ Promoter: High trust level, verbal skills

○ Relater: Team player, persistent, cooperative

○ Supporter: Accommodating, dislikes confrontation, adaptable

○ Coordinator: Self-disciplined, slow to change, pessimistic

○ Analyzer: Precise, accurate, nonverbal communicator

Not all styles are present in any given team, and many individuals possess a combination of styles. But whether a team is comprised of 4 people or 14, the players will not accomplish their goals without first understanding differences in style.

STRATEGY FOUR – OPEN YOUR MAP

Leadership is another term that's been exhausted to the point of cliché. I'll keep this simple, sparing you the countless analogies, historical references and anecdotes stuffed into other books and magazines. Good managers are good leaders, and good leaders **Make Action Possible (MAP)**. They map by:

1. Informing the "crew" about their ultimate destination;

2. Describing why this destination is an important objective;

3. Offering a road map to guide everyone to the final destination.

As a manager, you might declare, "By December of next year, I want to expand our operation to City X in order to exploit untapped opportunities and increase company-wide profits by 20%." How you get there is up to you. Do not insist that everyone use the same vehicles and follow the same route. Some employees will prefer the scenic route. Others will hop on the company jet. The means are less important than the ends. And so long as everyone understands the ends, you'll achieve your objectives.

The biggest problems occur when leaders roll up the map and tuck it into a desk drawer. The whole point is to keep it open. Keep the MAP open all of the time so everyone can refer to it all of the time and refresh their memories. And make sure your employees feel comfortable "stopping at the nearest gas station" to ask directions. Make yourself available, and offer your best suggestions – without making the person feel like an idiot for requesting help. Stick an "open" sign in your office if need be!

STRATEGY FIVE – MAKE USE OF ALL "FEEDBACK"

Managers receive feedback from a variety of sources. Informal feedback may come from direct reports, co-workers and supervisors during individual conversations. Customers provide feedback simply by interacting with your business and more formally through customer surveys. More recognized feedback is delivered through performance evaluations, employee surveys and assessment results. There is a lot to be learned by frequently reviewing feedback and looking for trends and key information. All forms of feedback should be reviewed. Some feedback should be taken more seriously. Consistent feedback requires immediate action.

13

I AM WHO TAUGHT ME

Every one of us is where we are today because someone helped us, taught us or pointed the way. Management is now embracing this belief. Companies and organizations are placing strong emphasis on people development through relationships. Succession planning programs are surfacing. Coaching strategies are being taught. Mentoring is encouraged and supported by management. Regardless of the business you're in, people – namely customers and employees – are its lifeblood.

I've found that many of us forget the impact that others have had on our success. Do we know the origin of our latest supporter? How did we meet him or her? Who was responsible for initiating the relationship? What would have happened if we had not met that person? I compare this process to creating a family tree.

THE SUCCESS TREE

This discovery led me to develop my "Success Tree™" exercise, which I use when teaching senior management mentoring and leadership skills. I ask all participants to trace the roots of relationships that impacted their careers or business successes. Here's how the process works:

YOUR SUCCESS TREE

○ Think of a recent success.

○ Identify the individual who helped you (directly or indirectly) to achieve this success.

○ Recall how you met this person.

○ Think of who initiated or facilitated this encounter. It could be an individual or a group.

○ Picture the circumstances that prompted your actions.

○ Continue this process as far back as you can remember.

○ Start this process over again by recalling other successful achievements.

While conducting a recent management workshop, I witnessed the impact of this process on the participants. I decided it was time again for me to draw another "Success Tree" of my own. The experience was powerful. I recalled people I hadn't spoken with in years. I remembered lessons painfully learned and the "teachers" who stood by me. I relived the support of an acquaintance who became a close friend, and of a client whose referral (five years earlier) continues to provide a steady source of income.

I began to contact my success sources. A few I could not locate. One had died. The rest were more than happy to hear from me. All were thrilled about my successes and pleased to recall the roles they'd played in my life. A surprising result of this effort – new doors opened, new relationships developed and a new lesson was learned. A former mentor, now 70-some years, told me, "You should go back to your tree more often. Every year it bears new fruit."

As you coach and mentor others while growing your business, use this method to subtly emphasize the importance of relationships to your success. Managers who use this process with their employees also discover a renewed team spirit and emphasis on the importance of each individual they have met.

FIVE SIMPLE PRINCIPLES

If I had to condense my employee engagement philosophy into a few simple principles, these are the ones I would highlight. Think of them as "The Five Commandments for Achieving Employee Engagement":

1. **Treat employees as individuals.** The more you know about the person and his or her life, the better you will understand the individual's behaviors, work patterns, job preferences and learning needs. This insight is a powerful communication and motivation tool. Build professional relationships. Inquire about their families. Get to know their favorite activities. Discuss current events. Seek their advice on particular challenges. Ask for their ideas and keep them involved in the business.

2. **Treat employees as adults.** As such, employees want control over their lives and work. Control means making decisions. Recognize this powerful motivator and use it. Don't assume that when an employee asks a question, it means he or she doesn't have an answer. Turn your answer into a question. "What's your opinion?" "How do you think this should be done?" By involving employees in the problem-solving process, you send a message that says, "You can do this!"

3. **Spur employee involvement.** Encourage employees to ask, "Why?" Questioning means involvement. Effective managers know that when their people are asking questions, they are thinking about their work and the company. These same managers also encourage healthy criticism and disagreement.

They actively listen and then ask for recommendations or solutions. Ownership begins with inquiries.

4. **Make employees partners.** People won't give their best if they don't understand the "how" and the "why" of their efforts. Of the companies we surveyed, 86% of managers and associates did not know their companies' general financial performance. Up to 65% of associates thought that the difference between an item's purchase price (wholesale) and retail price was net profit for the company. Many training programs do not address the financial basics of the business. Worse yet, many companies do not discuss profits or losses with associates, except as it relates to individual productivity. When employees are treated as partners in business, a sense of ownership, involvement and responsibility set in, and the pride in contribution fills a powerful personal need.

5. **Respect.** Uniqueness in people is celebrated. Differences are encouraged. Opinions are considered. When you give respect, you get respect. I once asked an employee to define respect. Her answer was simple: "I know when I feel it, and I know it when I don't."

Finally, please listen to your internal customer (employees) as diligently as you do external customers. Listening is all-important. No great idea ever enters the brain through the mouth!

14

THERE ARE NO RULES

Y ou may think the above sentiment is a cop out, but it's a valuable truth when it comes to dealing with human beings. When dealing with computers, you can enter an operation, instruct the computer to repeat when specified and count on an exact repetition of that operation every time you request it.

People aren't like that. Even if you discover a procedure that succeeds with a particular job applicant or employee, you can't count on obtaining reliable, reproducible results with all of the people. What works for one person may not work with anyone else!

I have included this caveat for one important reason. Any book designed to help you more effectively deal with people can only work when individual judgment is incorporated into the equations The study of human nature is not an exact science. How-to books and manuals on job profiling, behavioral assessments and job-to-employee matching can only offer guidelines, support, advice and counsel. At the heart of the pursuit for productivity in human resources is the word "human."

I once read *The Rules for Being Human*, for which the author is unknown. The impact on my own life has been immeasurable, so I'd like to share these rules with you.

THE RULES FOR BEING HUMAN

You will receive a body. You may like it or hate it, but it will be yours for the entire period this time around.

You will learn lessons. You are enrolled in a full-time informal school called *Life*. Each day in this school you will have the opportunity to learn lessons. You may like the lessons or think them irrelevant or stupid.

There are no mistakes, only lessons. Growth is a process of trial and error and experimentation. The "failed" experiments are as much a part of the process as the experiment that ultimately "works."

A lesson is repeated until learned. A lesson will be presented to you in various forms until you have learned it. When you have learned it, you can go on to the next lesson.

Learning lessons does not end. There is no part of life that does not contain its lessons. If you are alive, there are lessons to be learned.

"There" is no better than "here." When your "there" has become "here," you will simply obtain another "there" that will again look better than "here."

Others are merely mirrors of you. You cannot love or hate something about another person unless it reflects something you love or hate about yourself.

What you make of your life is up to you. You have all the tools and resources you need. What you do with them is up to you. The choice is yours.

Your answers lie inside you. The answers to life's questions lie inside you. All you need to do is look, listen and trust.

And…

You can remember the answers whenever you want.

Above all, respect birds for flying and fish for swimming. Our increasing capacity for engaging others should include an appreciation of many diverse talents and abilities. Turning the workforce into productive, satisfied and **engaged** individuals will profit everybody. It's only natural.

ABOUT THE AUTHOR

Terri Kabachnick is one of retailing's most sought-after productivity specialists and an international expert on "perfecting the human side of business." She founded The Kabachnick Group in 1984, and in more than 20 years of business has had the honor and privilege to work with some of the world's most successful business leaders.

Terri is frequently quoted as an employee behavior expert and has been featured in such publications as *USA Today*, numerous *Fairchild Publications, Chain Drug Review*, as well as other trade and industry publications. Her articles on communication and employee behaviors and beliefs have become required reading at many top companies.

A frequent keynote speaker at industry and trade conferences, Terri's motivational and informative presentations educate managers and executives in the behaviors, beliefs, attributes and competencies necessary for top performance and productivity. Terri frequently tells audiences: *"A business doesn't make people successful – people make the business successful."*

She is one of seven people worldwide to hold the following designations:

- CSP (Certified Speaking Professional)
- CPBA (Certified Professional Behavior Analysis)
- CPVA (Certified Professional Values Analyst)
- CAIA (Certified Attribute Index Analyst)

Additionally, Terri serves as coach and confidant to some of the world's most successful business leaders. She is the author of the Retail Interactive Coach, an interactive multimedia retail training program and STAR Performer – New Techniques in Retail Selling audio training program.

You can learn more by visiting **www.kabachnick.com** and **www.terrikabachnick.com.**

OTHER WAYS TO ATTACK DISENGAGEMENT

Keynote Presentations
Let author Terri Kabachnick inspire your organization with her customized lessons, examples and stories. Combined with audience participation, Terri delivers a compelling and motivating learning experience while helping your organization *attack the spreading virus of disengagement.*

"*In*gagement Boot Camp"
Passion, Personal Accountability and Performance

Values Fulfilled + Personal Accountability = Superior Performance

Discover what drives you and how you can discover what others value. Understand how your internal drivers affect others and what kind of environment you are creating subconsciously. Learn why those internal messages affect your accountability, delegation and decision-making.

"The Engaged Leader" – The Journey to Total Management Engagement
A complete management training and development certification process for building an engaged workforce. Includes a series of leadership briefings, assessments, management workshops, training for EA's (Engagement Advisors) and progress audits.

"Get Engaged" Executive Retreat
Gather your executives and join Terri at a 1- or 2-day offsite meeting to redefine your goals and align your strategies. You'll leave energized, ready to engage employees and take your organization to the next level!

Mem-Cards
Mem-Cards are a fast-reading and highly effective card-based product presenting impactful ideas and important insights. Use them to conduct short Mem-Cards meetings, focusing on one new card each day. Ask your staff how they would use today's tip to more effectively handle a situation or opportunity.

"Winners are committed to
'hang in there' long enough to win."

– David Cottrell

Reinforce your organization's values with a CornerStone poster, note card or desktop print!

*Commitment • Excellence • Teamwork • Passion
Attitude • Making the Difference • Integrity • Change
Perseverance • Focus • Courage • Press On*

See the entire collection at
www.CornerStoneLeadership.com

Accelerate Team Performance Package

The Next Level ... Leading Beyond the Status Quo provides insight and direction on what it takes to lead your team to a higher and greater Next Level. **$14.95**

Power Exchange – How to Boost Accountability & Performance in Today's Workforce This quick read offers practical strategies to help any leader boost accountability and performance in today's workforce. **$9.95**

Passionate Performance ... Engaging Minds and Hearts to Conquer the Competition offers practical strategies to engage the minds and heart of your team at home, work, church or community. Read it and conquer your competition! **$9.95**

Monday Morning Communications provides workable strategies to solving serious communications challenges. **$14.95**

180 Ways to Walk the Recognition Talk will help you provide recognition to your people more often and more effectively. **$9.95**

Lessons in Loyalty takes you inside Southwest Airlines to discover what makes it so different ... and successful. **$14.95**

The Manager's Coaching Handbook is a practical guide to improve performance from your superstars, middle stars and falling stars. **$9.95**

Start Right – Stay Right is every employee's straight talk guide to personal responsibility and job success. Perfect for every employee at every level. **$9.95**

Ouch! That Stereotype Hurts Regardless of your job title, you need to communicate with others to be successful. If you want to communicate respect through your message so that you can help build a workplace where all individuals feel included, this book is for you! **$12.95**

The Manager's Communication Handbook will allow you to connect with employees and create the understanding, support and acceptance critical to your success. **$9.95**

The CornerStone Perpetual Calendar, a compelling collection of quotes about leadership and life, is perfect for office desks, school and home countertops. **$14.95**

CornerStone Collection of Note Cards Sampler Pack is designed to make it easy for you to show appreciation for your team, clients and friends. The awesome photography and your personal message written inside will create a lasting impact. Pack of 12 (one each of all 12 designs) **$24.95**

Visit www.CornerStoneLeadership.com for additional books and resources.

YES! Please send me extra copies of *I Quit, But Forgot to Tell You*!

1-30 copies $14.95   31-100 copies $13.95   101+ copies $12.95

I Quit, But Forgot to Tell You!   ——— copies X ———   = $ ———

I Quit, But Forgot to Tell You! Companion Resources

PowerPoint® Presentation (downloadable)   ——— copies X $99.95   = $ ———

Additional Team Performance Books

Accelerate Team Performance Package   ——— pack(s) X $149.95   = $ ———
(Includes one copy of *I Quit* and all
products listed on previous page)

Other Books

_____   ——— copies X ———   = $ ———

_____   ——— copies X ———   = $ ———

_____   ——— copies X ———   = $ ———

Shipping & Handling $ ———

Subtotal $ ———

Sales Tax (8.25%-TX Only) $ ———

Total (U.S. Dollars Only) $ ———

Shipping and Handling Charges						
Total $ Amount	Up to $50	$51-$99	$100-$249	$250-$1199	$1200-$2999	$3000+
Charge	$6	$9	$16	$30	$80	$125

Name _____ Job Title _____

Organization _____ Phone _____

Shipping Address _____ Fax _____

Billing Address _____ Email _____
(required when ordering PowerPoint® Presentation)

City _____ State _____ ZIP _____

❏ Please invoice (Orders over $200) Purchase Order Number (if applicable) _____

Charge Your Order: ❏ MasterCard   ❏ Visa   ❏ American Express

Credit Card Number _____ Exp. Date _____

Signature _____

❏ Check Enclosed (Payable to: CornerStone Leadership)

Mail
Phone 888.789.5323   www.**CornerStoneLeadership**.com   P.O. Box 764087
Fax 972.274.2884   Dallas, TX 75376

CornerStone
Leadership Institute